Buying less for less...

What does that mean?

Too often good procurement pros have approached the marketing space with misguided goals. Self-assigned or otherwise, those goals have been to cut costs and reduce spending. After much diligent work, some think they succeed... but it is an illusion. They think they achieve buying more for less. But because talented people are the core of marketing costs, and talent costs what it costs, the new low prices actually translate into buyers *buying less for less*.

The marketing procurement dilemma is that the job isn't to *procure*; the job is to *invest*. Marketing is not a cost to be minimized. It's an investment to be maximized. When Procurement pros adopt the mindset of an investor, they contribute greatly, and CMOs and brands win. They succeed when they "invest" more and when they "buy" less.

Read on and discover exactly what's unique about procuring marketing services, and explore the four proven ways in which Marketing Procurement can help CMOs truly get *more for less*.

BUYING LESS
FOR LESS

How to avoid the Marketing Procurement dilemma

Gerry Preece
Russel Wohlwerth

buckdale
PUBLISHING

Buying Less for Less:
How to avoid the Marketing Procurement dilemma

Copyright © 2013
by Gerry Preece and Russel Wohlwerth
External View Consulting Group

Printed in the United States
Buckdale Publishing, Cincinnati, Ohio

ISBN: 978-0-98-54427-4-3

buckdale
PUBLISHING

CONTENTS

BUYING LESS FOR LESS

1: Clear Thinking and Straight Talk

A great advertising agency once wisely stated that the problem with most communications is that we round the things off to accommodate the crowd. We soften our sharp words, and we file down our prickly arguments so their edges are less grating. We collect input from the many and craft our words with careful precision so that everyone feels consulted and included. We drift inch by inch toward the twin goals of not giving offense and leaving ourselves a way out if we do. And in the process, we fail in our communications.

That is why we have deliberately chosen to write this in a direct and unambiguous fashion. We believe the message is too important to round off and too valuable to make fuzzy. We do not present the inputs of a representative cross-section of voices, nor do we average the various voices up as a way to water them down. We present here our unvarnished convictions, based on what we have witnessed through experience and know to be true. Of course we have consulted others and have digested industry information and survey data. But this work is not a repackaging of those things.

While we believe there is a place for averaging ideas from the many and for painstaking subtlety of language, we also believe these are the very reasons our industry has failed to make the right progress on the issue of Marketing Procurement. All constituents – Procurement, Marketing, and agencies – have had a lot to say. But until now, we have all been muddy in our thinking and in our arguments, and we've failed to make the right case to the right people.

The time has come to move beyond a democratic collection of voices, to get crystal clear in our thinking, and to map a winning way forward.

We aim our message toward Chief Marketing Officers, because they have the most to gain and lose in all this. Just as important, CMOs also have the ability to implement the solutions presented in this book. We expect CMOs will want to share the ideas in this book with Chief Procurement Officers, Chief Financial Officers, and key agency leaders, and we write with that in mind. Our objective is to make the right case to the right person, and empower the CMO to implement powerful solutions by working effectively with C-level leaders.

Although the "Marketing Procurement Issue" is a global problem, we have chosen to write this from a U.S. perspective. We do that simply because this geographical market continues to be the locus for many of our clients, and it is where we are based. That said, nearly every piece of analysis, every argument, and every string of logic found in this book applies globally.

I (Gerry) am an unabashed Proud Procurement Guy; I'm a zealot. I spent a decade practicing Marketing Procurement, and served as the Global Director of Marketing Procurement for the world's largest marketer, Procter & Gamble.[1] For the last several years I have consulted in this space, which has significantly expanded my exposure to a variety of marketers and agencies. Along the way I've learned a lot. I have also developed a profound respect for the remarkable power of marketing. I've seen Marketing Procurement work wonders in this space, and so I am an ardent believer. I've also seen it do terrible damage, and I want that to stop.

Russel has long been steeped in marketing, having served in McCann Erickson, as an executive at DDB, and ultimately as a respected consultant and industry insider. Like Gerry, Russel has seen Marketing Procurement add

---

[1] When I share my P&G background, I often hear comments about P&G's "rarified air." It is a sort of backhanded compliment. The notion is that P&G is an elite place that operates in lofty ways unattainable to mere mortal companies. But there is a subtle criticism and objection that accompanies the "rarified air" comment, and that criticism is its central message. It is a way of discounting the lesson, a way of dismissing it. "It might work in the unique and special environment at P&G, but it won't work out here in the real world," the idea goes. Really? I wonder how unique and rarified P&G's air really is. I just took a look at stock price indices for the last five years and compared P&G to some major competitors: Unilever, Colgate, Kimberly-Clark, Johnson & Johnson, Kraft, Clorox, Kao, and a few others. P&G didn't outperform a single one of them. Maybe P&G's got "regular" air, just like everyplace else. It also doesn't take long to find ex-P&G managers who are now in key leadership roles at literally dozens of great companies, from direct competitors to Microsoft to Coca Cola to Levi Strauss, and on and on. Apparently somebody saw some value in their experiences. Maybe lessons from P&G, just like lessons from IBM, Ford, Google, and Costco might be relevant to "regular air" places after all. Good lessons are good lessons, and they can make a difference anywhere.

great value – and he's seen it be disastrous.

As an industry we drone on about how things are still not right regarding Procurement. We wring our hands and watch helplessly as nothing seems to get better. Some have even come to accept today's awkward Marketing Procurement Malaise as the industry's "new normal." Not us.

When it comes to Marketing Procurement, the time has finally come to get it right. The good news is that getting it right isn't particularly hard. It just requires clear thinking and straight talk.

Indeed, CMOs *can* get more for less. They just need four things that have consistently proven to deliver great results in this space. These are the "4 proven ways CMOs can get more for less." This formula works, and it is repeatable. CMOs need this from Procurement:

1. People with the **right mindset,**
2. measured by the **right metrics,**
3. applying the **right skills,**
4. in the **right assignments.**

This book is laid out in a clear and methodical way, and it builds the case, piece by piece, as to why these four proven ways constitute the right solution. We'll explain exactly why Procurement belongs in the marketing space, and we'll also make the clear case for why Procurement has to take a different approach in marketing.

Let's begin by clarifying exactly what the problem is (and what it is not).

2: The Problem

Perhaps no problem has ever been more misstated or misdiagnosed. Frustrations run high, and complaints and accusations are everywhere in our industry. They appear regularly in trade journals, in the halls of agency buildings, and marketer conference rooms. The Marketing Procurement Problem made the "Book of 10's List" for *Advertising Age's* 2010 Year in Review edition, in which the top ten topics for the year were listed. The complaints still pop up at nearly every Association of National Advertisers (ANA) or American Association of Advertising Agencies (4A's) gathering, and they can be heard at Procurement events everywhere.

They're just afraid we're going to make them look bad! Procurement doesn't understand marketing! They're too focused on cost savings! Marketing doesn't get what Procurement can do for them! Agencies charge too much and are irresponsible with client money!

The list of complaints goes on and on, and sadly, we have come to treat each of these things as "the problem." They are not. We have substituted stating the complaint for clarifying the problem. We've gotten muddled in our thinking and unclear about the distinctions between problem and symptoms. We have even gone so far as to study each complaint in detail and have put corrective actions in place, all well-intended. And all ineffective. That's because none of these things are really the core cause for our predicament. They do represent important issues, but they are not the real problem.

To understand the real problem, and to put these other important issues in context, we first have to understand some history and our current state.

Marketing Procurement – Where They're Coming From

As far back as the 1980s and 1990s, a small number of marketing companies had their procurement people involved in the procurement of marketing goods and services. In those early days Procurement concerned itself with commodities that looked and felt like the direct materials items (items that go into Cost of Goods Sold, which they had been buying for decades). These were generally things like printed materials and premiums, things that lent themselves to clear specifications and which required little creativity. Price was the great (and sometimes the only) differentiator. Being skilled and professional buyers, Procurement delivered measureable results. Procurement scorecards reflected the savings contributions from these "new spend areas," and procurement leaders began to secretly salivate over the untapped potential they saw in all those additional marketing dollars which had traditionally been considered off limits to them.

With time and familiarity, pleased marketers invited Procurement, complete with their resumes of savings in printed materials and premiums, to take cautious steps into additional marketing spend areas. They began to get involved with things like coupons, telemarketing services, and mailing lists, which were a little more complex. Small results led to bigger ones, and inch by inch, Procurement advanced into additional marketing spend areas. But this is also the era in which things began to get awkward between Procurement and Marketing, and eventually between Procurement and agencies. Some procurement folks pushed hard for savings, while others began to adjust to the uniqueness of marketing, a spend area in which not all value arrived in the form of price.

Ultimately, after the new millennium arrived, some procurement groups were getting directly involved with agency selections and fee negotiations. Other marketers looked around and wondered aloud why their procurement organizations weren't in the marketing game yet. They feared they were falling behind, and the floodgates began to open. Marketing procurement organizations weren't just for the few anymore; they were becoming increasingly common. All this eventually produced the broad-based marketplace phenomenon of Marketing Procurement that we have before us today.

It can be said that those procurement organizations that led the way deserved to make the inroads they did. That's because their advancement into marketing was earned, and along the way they learned valuable lessons about how to do the work. Those procurement organizations that came later, and perhaps especially those that came via fiat and mandate, often arrived without the benefit of years of hard-earned experience in the marketing space. As a result, some marketing procurement groups were recognized as being strong, while some others were thought of as destructive to overall marketing efforts. The seeds of conflict were sown here, and constituents (Procurement, Marketing, and agencies) retreated to their respective camps in defense of their own interests.

Procurement, under assault and sensing a need to defend itself, accused marketers of feeling threatened by Procurement's superior buying skills. They accused agencies of fearing accountability. Marketers accused Procurement of not understanding marketing and damaging delicate and critical creative relationships. And agencies accused Procurement of heavy-handed price slashing that ultimately hurt their industry and their clients. There was a nugget of truth, and maybe more than that, in what all of them were saying. So where are we now?

Procurement: "The Good, the Bad, and the Ugly"

In 2010 the ANA published the findings of a study entitled *"Procurement: The Good, the Bad, and the Ugly."* It was a comprehensive, sixty-two page report on the research they had conducted in conjunction with the 4A's.[2] The marketer side and the agency side combined resources to assess

---

[2] Association of National Advertisers (ANA). American Association of Advertising Agencies (4A's).

exactly how things were going with Procurement, a still relatively new but increasingly powerful force in the world of marketing and agencies.

Considering that as an industry, we had been working on this for years, the results were downright awful. Worse, the findings of the study included a particularly bad surprise. Nearly everyone expected the survey results to show how fractured things were between agencies and Procurement, but few expected to see the disconcerting rift between Marketing and their own procurement organizations. The problems were broad based and included everything from Procurement being too focused on cutting costs, to not sufficiently understanding marketing, to the negative ways in which Procurement interacts with agencies. The results were disappointing and sobering at best, and at worst, a condemnation of what some hoped would finally be declared a failed experiment. After about a decade of Procurement being "on the map" in marketing, it seemed little progress had been made.

Two major initiatives came out of this work. The ANA commissioned a task force to address the issues and provide direction, and it also established a cross-advertiser mentoring program to help new procurement people. Both are noble causes. However, some recent research we conducted (less extensive than the ANA study but nevertheless a fair snapshot of the marketplace) indicates there has been little change in the bottom line findings.[3] So here we are today,

---

[3] Russel Wohlwerth of External View conducted a 2011 survey of over one hundred industry players. Our unscientific study found that the situation was still remarkably bad. Procurement was not seen as a good ally; they were not seen as being sufficiently skilled or as adequately understanding the value of marketing;

still wrestling with "The Marketing Procurement Issue."

There are some who believe Procurement should just go away. To one degree or another, they believe Procurement is bad for marketing – bad for both agencies and for the marketers they purport to represent. Their experience has been that Procurement cuts costs to the point of damage and that the ultimate outcome is weaker marketing and weaker client brands. They see no upside, only negatives. Some in this camp say these things out loud. But most share it only in private, as it has become a politically charged topic and there can be repercussions for those who too openly dissent.

A second group essentially sees no problem. This group mostly consists of procurement people themselves, but a few marketers are here as well. Generally speaking, this group believes that agencies are sloppy with the client's money, that agencies are wasteful and unaccountable, and that the way to move the needle here is with direct pressure on agencies. Like the first group, they find it dangerous to speak their minds too clearly. And because of that, this group is often perceived as saying one thing and doing another. "Of course agencies are our partners," they'll say. But then they conduct a fee negotiation that is anything but collaborative.

Finally, there is a group that believes Procurement has an important and valuable role to play but has yet to find it. This camp struggles with how to properly integrate Procurement so as to take advantage of the good they can bring, while at the same time eliminating the pitfalls of "the bad" and "the ugly." People in this camp see Procurement doing good work in many diverse industries, and they think

they were seen as focusing to a fault on cost cutting; and they were often seen as damaging the effectiveness of agency outputs.

that done the right way, Procurement can help in marketing too. They are bolstered by the knowledge that indeed there are some marketing procurement organizations that are well regarded and that add value, that deliver on "the good."

I (Gerry) count myself in this latter group. I am a believer. I am also a realist. I believe because I lived it, because I headed Procter & Gamble's Global Marketing Purchases organization for a number of years. I believe it because I saw firsthand what worked and what didn't. I believe because I experienced real and dramatic benefits for client marketers that didn't damage agencies, and because I witnessed remarkable agency improvements that didn't come at the expense of clients. I learned how procurement skills could be applied in powerful ways, ways in which brands grew and agency capabilities were enhanced. Just as important, I also made enormous mistakes. I botched negotiations and practiced naiveté and saw brands (and agencies) hurt. Before I learned to apply good metrics, I applied metrics that caused damage. I put the wrong people in the wrong jobs and at times set the wrong agenda. In my decade of doing marketing procurement for the world's largest marketer, and in my subsequent years consulting in this space, I have learned a lot. Above all, I became profoundly convinced that Procurement has tremendous potential to add value in the world of marketing, and if not managed properly, a tremendous potential to cause harm.

So how do we move forward? As with any problem, we have to start by accurately defining exactly what the problem is.

The Real Problem

Despite this confusing mix of symptoms and issues, there indeed is one overarching issue, one central problem from which everything else proceeds. As an industry, we have suffered from a collective failure to keep this one issue at the forefront. We have given in to the temptation to seize on this symptom or that one, on one sub-problem or another. Along the way we have become distracted by a variety of concerns which, though real, miss the central point. Because of that failure, the various sub-issues float out there like independent satellites, seemingly unconnected to one another, and un-tethered to the one core problem, the one and only thing that gives them relevance.

There is truth in the claim that Procurement often fails to sufficiently understand marketing, but that is not the main problem. It is justifiable to say that Procurement is frequently too focused on cost savings, but that is not the core issue. It's valid to claim that Marketing sometimes doesn't understand Procurement's skill set and therefore fails to leverage Procurement's capabilities, but that is not the primary problem. It's true that agencies are often too inattentive to cost controls, but that is not the fundamental problem. Procurement doesn't understand. Marketing is undisciplined. Agencies are fat and happy. Procurement asks the wrong questions and applies the wrong processes. Marketing is too guarded and defensive. The agency costs too much and isn't leading our thinking. The list of issues and complaints goes on and on. But none of these things are the real problem.

There is only one problem that really matters, only one problem that deserves to be solved. Every other concern needs to be subordinated to this one; every potential solution to every sub-problem has to satisfy this one, central need. The only problem that really matters is this: *Marketing dollars are limited. They are finite. There is a broad, universal need for every CMO to become increasingly efficient with the limited marketing resources that are available, and that translates into an unending pressure to do more with less.* **The real problem is that we have to increase marketing ROI.**

If we keep this goal in mind – and only if we keep it in mind – we can solve the various sub-problems like those mentioned above. It's not about turf wars or egos. It's not about "fixing" any of the groups or players involved. It's about improving marketing efficiency – period. As soon as we lose focus on this, we get ourselves in trouble.

With this one core problem clearly defined as the objective, we are then able to tackle three essential sub-problems that will enable success. First, we have to establish in a convincing way why Procurement belongs in the game. Second, we have to make the compelling case that marketing really is a unique space that requires a unique approach from Procurement. And third, we have to clearly spell out the logical implications for Procurement's approach, and translate those into actionable steps.

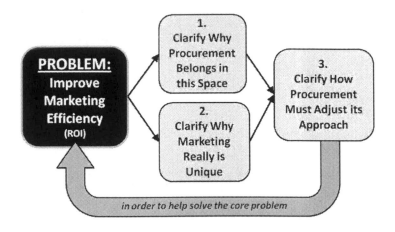

If we do these things well – with clear thinking and straight talk – we will make good progress toward our goal, which is to improve marketing ROI. We've seen it work. It can be the magic ingredient, the philosopher's stone that turns things into gold. But Procurement has to engage in the right way. When it's done the wrong way, it can do serious damage, and that means there are times when Procurement should not be in the game. We must be crystal clear about what works and what doesn't – and why.

So let's start at the beginning. Why should Procurement even be in the marketing space in the first place?

3: The Case for Procurement

The first and most significant point that needs to be made here is that **it's not about the function; it's about the skills.** It's not about involving "Procurement," it's about engaging and applying skills that can and will make a difference. Our lack of clarity on this one issue is responsible for years of frustration and many failures, and it has led to faulty conclusions and many missed opportunities. Finally getting ourselves clear on this one single distinction will work wonders in moving us toward a solution.

So we will *not* make a case for Procurement. We *will* make a case for strategic sourcing. We'll get back to Procurement soon enough.

Relevant Skills: Strategic Sourcing

These skills definitely apply in the marketing space, and in most cases they are desperately needed. Strategic sourcing is codified in different ways in different organizations, but just as you expect professional sales people to have a methodology for strategically selling, you can also expect professional procurement people to have a methodology for strategically buying. In its simplest form, strategic sourcing has five basic components that form a continuous, ongoing process.[4]

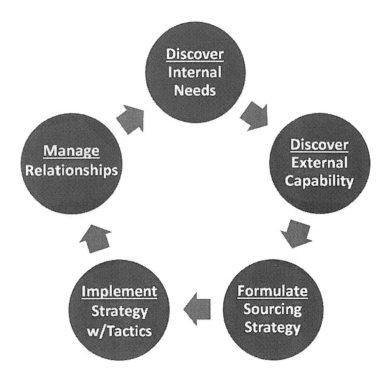

Basic Strategic Sourcing Model

---

[4] There are entire books written on the topic of strategic sourcing, and all of its five elements are densely packed with principles and content. External View and others offer such training and assist with building great marketing procurement organizations. This book, intended to serve as a guide for CMOs, provides only a very high level description of the skill set.

Discover internal needs – While this sounds simple enough, it is often surprisingly complex. That's because internal clients commonly only ask for what they have been receiving or what they expect to receive from outside vendors/suppliers/agencies. A skilled sourcer will get them to go deeper, to share their wish lists and "wildest dreams." There's often a big difference between what clients really want and what they think they can ask for – and good strategic sourcers have learned to uncover a client's true needs and wants. This can lead to breakthroughs and important innovation.

Beyond this, a good practitioner will find common needs and aggregate them where it makes sense. He will think three to five years into the future, and will develop a picture of where his marketing organization is going, so that he can better match the organization's long term marketing needs with what the agency industry has to offer, both for today and for tomorrow.

Discover external market capabilities – Good strategic sourcers are experienced evaluators of outside companies and markets. They have typically visited dozens of businesses and assessed each company's capabilities relative to others. They know how to ask for references and how to discern between the accolades of demanding customers and the faint praises of submissive ones. Good strategic sourcers have learned what questions to ask about financial status and legal entanglements; they have learned to pick up subtle but relevant nuances of organizational culture; and they have deep experience making objective, thorough,   side-by-side comparisons of outside businesses.

They develop well-informed, thoughtful perspectives on the industry, and they can identify the key distinctions and differences between suppliers/agencies. Equally as important, they are able to pick out the distinctions that matter, the ones that make a difference when considered against the long term internal needs. This knowledge informs the sourcing strategy they will develop.

Formulate a customized sourcing strategy – You can expect good sourcers to define a strategic marketplace approach based on the two factors above. Internal needs and external capabilities will lead them to a thoughtful strategy regarding how to proceed. The sourcing strategy will answer a number of things. Should we buy for six months or three years? Should we buy from one source or from many? One global solution or several local ones? Fees or commissions or flat rate? Do we take a partnership approach, or do we stay arms-length and distant? Bid or negotiate? Holding company model or independent agency model? Do we care if the other party makes money? Etc.

Good sourcing strategies are neither right nor wrong. Instead, they make clear philosophical choices and they clearly articulate why each philosophical choice is made. Sourcing strategies serve as a roadmap and as an alignment tool. They provide a clear way forward, and they allow leaders to align the organization in powerful ways.

The best strategic sourcers, having deeply assessed internal needs and uncovered unmet desires, use that knowledge to influence the external marketplace, to reshape it in ways that bring true advantage to their internal clients. This intentional shaping of the external marketplace is a deliberate and proactive step; it is an act of strategy and leadership.

Implement the strategy using relevant tactics – Next, the strategy has to be implemented with skill and expertise. Internal marketers have to be consulted. Agencies have to be assessed. Bids or negotiations have to be conducted. Appropriate contracts and controls have to be put in place. RFIs, RFPs, management of the commercial aspects of one-time projects, back-up and contingency sourcing plans, and the like all have to be managed professionally. Good strategic sourcing folks do these things well.

Each of these tactics represents an entire set of specialized skills, and good sourcers are well grounded in all of them. As just one example, they are skilled negotiators. They know how to prepare for a negotiation and how to open the negotiation. They know which side should go first. They know how to make a concession and how to demand one from the other side. They know when to walk away and how to do it. They know how to answer objections and how to argue for the outcomes they want. They know how to close the negotiation, how to lock it down, and how to hold the other guy accountable. The same kind of skill depth applies to contracts and RFPs and every other relevant tactic/activity.

Manage the ongoing commercial relationship – Just as sales people manage relationships with their customers, good strategic sourcing talent manages commercial relationships with external suppliers and agencies. This is done deliberately and with intention, and it is an ongoing effort. It involves agency evaluations and feedback sessions, management of expectations regarding commercial considerations, continuous improvement of systems and processes, and more.

Good strategic sourcers know the leaders and key decision makers on the supplier/agency side, and they develop relationships that have a foundation of respect and trust. The best sourcer wants to be able to call in a favor when the chips are down, and she wants to be able to deliver a tough message when it needs to be heard and acted upon. These kinds of relationships take time and deliberate effort, and they don't happen over a single lunch meeting.

Smart strategic sourcers are careful to lead on the commercial relationship and to have Marketing lead on the work of marketing. The two efforts are unique but closely related. When it's done well, the efforts are synergistic.

Progress on this step leads directly back to reassessing internal needs, and the cycle continues.

* * * * *

These skills are desperately needed in most marketing companies. Their absence produces the all too common symptoms: agencies assigned to areas outside of their sweet spot, misaligned and mismanaged client-agency relationships, frustrated marketers and bewildered agencies. CMOs end up feeling that they are paying too much for too little in the way of results. CMOs want agencies to lead their thinking, and they become frustrated that it's not happening. Line marketers become disappointed because the agency is not giving them what they want fast enough or at the prices they think are fair.

Agencies come to feel whip-sawed. They hunger for clear briefs and strategic direction and the end of micro-management by clients. They want to do great work, but feel the constant pressure to meet arbitrarily low and unsustainable price levels. They fear they will be fired at any moment, and they have no idea if they fit into the client's long term plans.

The overall keyword becomes *misalignment*. People on all sides start to feel like the system – that is the way they work and are compensated and evaluated and rewarded – just doesn't match up with the reality of their daily demands. Marketers are accountable for today's results, but the agency seems focused on tomorrow. Agencies hear loud and clear that the client wants great insights, but there is no budget for research, and Procurement is demanding even lower rates. You know how this goes; you live it every day....

And then there is the worst symptom of all: weak marketing.

The above skills listed above aren't a panacea; they won't magically solve every ailment. But without systematically applying these kinds of skills, marketers don't have a prayer of succeeding on a sustained basis. Marketing ROI won't get better. Without applying these skills, marketers will stay in the do-loops of disappointment and frustration. They will recycle agency after agency, firing at will and chasing an elusive, un-catchable mirage of marvelous marketing. Things will be even worse if they stumble on success now and then, which cruelly lends momentary credibility to the lie that the approach is okay, that we all just have to work a little harder... the truth is that they just won't get there.

But if these strategic sourcing skills are engaged, you will see a more coherent approach to agency selection, agency assignments, compensation, agency performance and relationship management. When an organization applies these skills to the marketing space, there is a more logical and deliberate approach to how agencies are selected and engaged. There is an overall strategy that makes sense regarding which agencies to use and how to use them. There is consistency and rationale as to how they are compensated and evaluated. Agencies end up with clearer priorities, and people on both sides are more aligned. Applying the skills produces systemic improvements, and they drive a healthy and constructive amount of operational rigor. Things like agency briefing processes become more routine and efficient, and they enable better, faster, cheaper results. Project management practices improve, affecting things like approvals and the management of revisions. Role clarity, process clarity, and the effective management of expectations removes agency anxiety and allows them to be better, faster, more efficient, and more creative. And at the same time, it helps client-side marketers to develop faster and produce better results.

Smart application of strategic sourcing skills will help any CMO get more for less. It will help improve marketing ROI.

When to NOT use Procurement in Marketing

If your Procurement organization doesn't do these kinds of things well, if they aren't strategic sourcing practitioners or skilled professionals, then a new question arises: what skills *do* they bring that are relevant? CMOs should get a clear and satisfying answer to this question before proceeding with Procurement's involvement. This is not the time for wishful thinking or polite concessions. If Procurement doesn't bring relevant skills to the table, they have no business influencing sourcing decisions in the marketing spend area. If they are only order processers, run for the hills. If they are process managers with a slavish dedication to structured bidding that's designed to reduce costs, bar them from entry. If they parachute in, run their standardized process, and then jump back out of the picture, circle the wagons and send them away.

Just as the laws of bell curve distributions apply to agencies and marketing teams, they also apply to procurement organizations. If the procurement team falls short on strategic sourcing skills, you can consider several options. One is to simply proceed without them, but this does nothing to engage the skills you still need. A second choice is to help Procurement develop these skills, and there are outside resources (like External View) that specialize in this work. And third, consider engaging outside resources directly, as they can bring these skills to bear (see Appendix, "The Case for Consultants").

Our intent here is not to disparage procurement organizations that might be light on strategic sourcing skills. Keep in mind that Procurement gets called on to do a lot more than just strategic sourcing, and it's possible that for whatever reason, the other work has been their strategic focus for years. The point is simply that CMOs should be seeking strategic sourcing skills, and some procurement organizations are naturally going to be stronger at this; others will be weaker.

Always remember that it's not about involving "Procurement," it's about applying these critical and relevant skills.

A Word about Controls

Many good procurement organizations have a complimentary set of skills that we will call "purchasing administration." It's a critically important skill set. It's every bit as essential as strategic sourcing, but it's a very different animal. Purchasing administration involves a systematic approach to managing transactions across the internal organization and with outside suppliers. It's about managing budgets, insuring that orders and invoices and payments are all valid, and providing the appropriate accountability and controls to the spend area. There are layers and depths of sophistication in purchasing administration, just as there are for strategic sourcing.

We raise this here only to insure C-level awareness of the distinction, so that CMOs and others can categorize the various skills in relevant ways. CMOs should want purchasing administration in their space. It helps provide good controls, and that's good business. It's often the best place for strategic sourcing people to start, because it can provide an excellent picture of the current reality regarding marketing suppliers and agency work. But CMOs also need to be clear that purchasing administration skills won't solve the business issues described earlier.

Strategic Sourcing	Purchasing Administration
Longer term, External focus	Shorter term, Internal focus
Spend Analyses	Purchase Orders/ Controls
Needs Assessments	Budget allocations,
Strategy & Implementation	Invoices & Payments,
Relationship management	Authorizations & Approvals

An Impressive Track Record

Forty years ago, Procurement was what some would have called a fringe profession. Some companies treated Procurement as a valued function, complete with the trappings of skills training, deliberate career development planning, and recruitment and succession plans. But very often, Procurement roles represented sideline opportunities for good people who for various reasons wanted out of other, more mainstream roles. Procurement people were often self-taught specialists, learning their trade through experience and with the aid of one or two industry associations.

How things have changed. Professional procurement people got much deserved recognition for their heroics in the U.S. auto industry in the 1980's, and that put Procurement on the map in a new way. Desperate to save their failing companies, Chief Procurement Officers and senior buyers famously tore up long term supplier contracts and did these things publically, in the full light of day. Instead of asking suppliers for quotes, they turned the game upside down and *told* the vendors what the prices would be. "Hit price X or we fire you and buy from the other guy," they said. And they did… and it worked. They invented the whole idea of target pricing. If it weren't for Procurement (and some of their heavy-handed tactics) some auto companies would undoubtedly have folded. They saved the day. Suddenly Procurement was in the *Wall Street Journal* and in all the business magazines.

At the same time, outsourcing was becoming a widespread practice, and businesses shed tasks that didn't line up with their core competencies. Procurement was leveraged in these new spend areas, and began inching its way into new territories, despite the reluctance of various internal clients. Once strictly concerned with only direct materials, Procurement began moving into a number of indirect spend areas, such as office supplies, janitorial services, food service, travel, and more.

Procurement did good work, and the savings piled up. In spend pool after spend pool, Procurement registered impressive successes. They broke what were effectively supplier cartels and monopolistic models. Cost improvements of twenty or thirty percent were not unusual. CFOs began to embrace the trend because of the savings and because Procurement's methodical approach allowed for better controls.

Emboldened by their own successes, Procurement seized new ground after new ground. They were getting recognized in board rooms where only a couple of decades earlier, such accolades for the Procurement function would have seemed impossible. They were being elevated, and rightly so. They were becoming more high profile. They were delivering when their companies needed it most. And finally they came to set their sights on the one remaining spend pool that had to that point remained off limits to them: marketing.

Why "We're Different" Doesn't Resonate

Procurement's migration into each of the aforementioned new spend pools wasn't always welcomed. They weren't often received with open arms. Quite the opposite. In spend pool after spend pool, incumbent managers (who were effectively functioning as buyers) resisted Procurement's participation. For example, if food service contracts were managed by the dining managers, they viewed the approach of Procurement as an invasion. How could they have felt otherwise? An important part of their job was being usurped. Pieces of their power floated away with it. Worse yet, it was being relinquished to people who (to put it politely) didn't know food service the way a food service professional did.

And so the cry went out. "This isn't direct materials! It's food service. You can do those procurement things over there, sure... but we're different!" The resistance was understandable and intentions were sincere. Food service managers, who were deeply schooled in the details of food service, had a tough time wrapping their mind around the idea that there was a science and methodology to buying things – and they had been buying things. They feared that professional procurement people, being unschooled in the science and methodology of food service, would make a terrible mess of things. Yet in the vast majority of cases, those fears never played out. Procurement procured and left the work of managing food service to the professionals. They came to trust one another and collaborated, and in the end, costs came down while food service performance went up.

Food services. Office supplies. Travel services. Distribution services. Facilities management services.

Procurement marched on, penetrating indirect spend pool after indirect spend pool. And in spend pool after spend pool they notched successes and contributions that CFOs and senior managers lauded. At every turn, Procurement met resistance. At every turn, they were derided. At every turn, they were told that their tactics and practices from direct materials would be disastrous if applied in this new spend pool. At every turn they were told, "but we're different!" Yet in spend pool after new spend pool, Procurement succeeded. In spend pool after new spend pool, results went to the bottom line, and the world did not end.

The cumulative lesson for Procurement became this: Procurement methodologies are indeed universal. There is such a thing as a Procurement skill set, and it can be reapplied successfully from spend pool to spend pool. And all you people who think your area is different... well, it's not so different after all.

So when Procurement hears Marketing say, "we're different," it bounces off their ears. They've heard it a hundred times before, and they simply no longer believe it.

4: BUT... Marketing Really IS Different

Making the Right Case to the Right People

We can bellow from the hilltops that marketing is different, but that won't deter Procurement. We can say until we're blue in the face that marketing is different; we can repeat it endlessly; we can yell it more loudly than ever. None of that will change a thing, for all the reasons described in the previous section. The proof is all around us. "Marketing is different" has been the wrong battle cry for years, and it has been utterly ineffective.

To make a difference, we have to do two things. First, we have to explain in detail exactly why and how marketing really *IS* different. We have to get specific. We have to be thorough. We have to provide bulletproof logic. And we have to articulate the rationale in terms that will have meaning for Procurement. We can't use marketing-speak for this critical task; we must use procurement-speak. We have to talk to Procurement in terms that they understand and care about. We have to explain what's different in terms that are relevant to Procurement.

Second, we must make the case to the people who can affect the necessary changes. Too often, marketers and agencies have pushed on the procurement person in the trenches, trying to convince the Procurement foot soldier that they are fighting the wrong war. That approach has never worked, and it doesn't work in this case either. The foot solder cannot change his or her remit. They cannot change their metrics or their deliverables or their scorecards. These are the things, as we will soon see, that have to change. And so we must make the case to the C-level people that can indeed implement the necessary changes.

Ten Big Reasons Why Marketing Really IS Different

Perhaps nothing in this book is more important than this section. If we fully grasp how and why marketing is indeed a uniquely different space, then we open the door to discuss how Procurement's approach in marketing needs to be different than the approach they take in other markets. But if Procurement doesn't grasp that marketing is different, if they don't accept that, then nothing can change.

Marketing really is different, and there are ten fundamental reasons why:

Expense vs. Investment	
Direct Materials Procurement	**Marketing Procurement**
We grudgingly spend "Cost "or "Expense" money	*Marketing is an "Investment" we embrace because it grows the business*

Marketing is an investment, not a cost – Nothing is more self-evident yet more ignored. Marketing money isn't being spent because we have to spend it. It's not a cost of doing business. There's nothing mandatory about a marketing budget. We spend money on marketing because we believe it adds value to our brands and to our top and bottom lines. If we don't believe those things, we should immediately stop spending the money. Nothing is easier than cutting costs in marketing: just stop spending! Cut the budget and boom – pocket the savings, problem solved. It's that simple.[5]

Who in their right mind makes an investment decision based primarily on the cost? Who buys a share of Microsoft because it's cheaper than a share of Coca-Cola? Who buys copper futures because copper's price per pound is cheaper than the price per pound of silver? Who invests in an original painting because it's cheaper than the other original painting hanging next to it? So why do we even engage in a discussion about things like agency or marketing supplier

---

[5] CMOs need to know that not all leaders believe marketing is a good investment. See the section entitled "Be Prepared: A Dirty Little Secret," on page 61.

costs and fees without at the same time discussing quality and market impact? Focusing on the cost of marketing services while ignoring future returns and benefits is pure lunacy.

The entire mindset needs to be different in Marketing Procurement. We're not trying to minimize costs; we're trying to maximize an investment. That bears repeating: **It's not about minimizing costs; it's about maximizing an investment.**[6]

Specifications & Quality	
Direct Materials Procurement	**Marketing Procurement**
Specifications are fixed and binary (go/no-go)	*Specifications are fluid, and quality is a variable*

Specifications are not fixed; they are fluid; and quality is a variable – Unlike almost anything else Procurement buys, it's impossible to write a specification for creative marketing services. Quality cannot be fixed like it can be with direct materials. With direct materials we write detailed, exacting specifications. They are binary, yes/no, go/no-go things. The

---

[6] We are troubled that the industry still calls it "Marketing Procurement." Any marketer can tell you that if you want to change a way people think about something, change its name. What would happen if we called it "Marketing Investment Management?" That would be much more reflective of what the job really is.

item in question is either in-spec or it isn't. Procurement simply can't choose to buy an off-quality truckload of stuff. They are not allowed, and all kinds of systemic checks and balances (like quality tests) make sure those off-quality buys never happen.

In direct materials, the mind of the buyer works like this: As long as I'm buying from in-spec, qualified sources, a truckload of Chemical X from one company is as good a truckload of Chemical X from the next company.

Not so when we look at things like a television media plan, a marketing campaign, a digital promotion, a direct mail program, qualitative market research, a print ad, a branded visual equity property, or a thousand other purchased items/services in the world of marketing. In the marketing space, Procurement can indeed source a solution that is dramatically different than other viable choices. In marketing, good stuff and bad stuff is all "in-spec," and the buyer can choose worse stuff or better stuff at will. Yes, there are a few marketing spend areas that do lend themselves to clearer specifications (e.g. some premiums, some print programs, some direct mail lists), but they represent relatively small dollars, and they are entwined with marketing spend areas that are not specifiable. They are the rare exception, not the rule.

Generally speaking, marketing services cannot be "specified." Therefore no two supplier/agency proposals can be considered on an apples-to-apples basis. In marketing, quality is a variable.

Ramifications of Buyer Decisions	
Direct Materials Procurement	*Marketing Procurement*
No significant differences in the quality of in-spec purchase choices	*The consequences of one "in-spec" purchase choice vs. another can be enormous*

The consequences of one "in-spec" purchase choice vs. another can be enormous – Not only are specs impossible to write in the marketing space; not only can a marketing services buyer legitimately buy one solution that differs significantly in quality from other choices; not only are those differences in quality difficult to assess while making the sourcing decision... But the consequences of making Legitimate Sourcing Choice A versus Legitimate Sourcing Choice B can be enormous – even several times the value of the sourcing decision itself.

Let's say you have a business with $10 million in revenue and a 10% profit margin. So you make $1 million/yr. Let's also say you're the Marketing Procurement person and you're in the process of hiring a general market creative/ad agency to help lead the marketing work. You work with your marketing team to write an excellent Statement of Work, and two agencies bid on it. Orange Agency quotes a fee of $40K and Apple Agency offers a fee of $100K. Apple is more than double the cost of Orange. They're both "in-spec." They're both on your qualified vendor list. Which do you buy?

	Orange Agency	Apple Agency	Difference
Fee/Cost	$40K	$100K	$60K ($60K spread)

What if one year later Apple Agency drove a 15% lift in your business. Great marketing can do that, and it's not uncommon. Also assume you have a profit margin of 40% on incremental sales (fixed costs like overhead and facilities have already been covered). That 15% lift translates to $600K in incremental profit. By contrast, what if one year later Orange Agency's marketing solutions resulted in a 3% decline in your business. Poor marketing can do this, and it's not uncommon. This scenario means a $120K decline in profits. The difference is $720K. Which agency do you wish you had signed up with?

	Orange Agency	Apple Agency	Difference
Fee/Cost	$40K	$100K	$60K ($60K spread)
End of Year Result	-3% Revenues (-$300K)	+15% Revenues (+$1,500K)	$1,800K (18% swing)
Impact on Profits	-$120K	+600K	$720K (14.4% vs. current base)
Investment Outcome	-$160K/yr and a smaller business	+$500K/yr and a bigger business	$660K and growing vs. shrinking business

Do the math for your own company or your own brands. Plug in realistic agency fee figures and approximate margins on incremental sales. In almost every realistic scenario, the impact of the resulting sales/profit at the end of the year will dwarf the spread in agency fees/costs. In other words, the consequences of one "in-spec" purchase choice versus another can be enormous. It doesn't mean we should ignore agency costs and fees; it means we need to think about the reason we're investing and keep fees in the proper context.

Legitimate, valid Marketing Procurement decisions can really hurt the business – or they can really help. They can impact the top line and the bottom line in ways Procurement decisions in direct materials cannot.

Supplier Differentiation	
Direct Materials Procurement	*Marketing Procurement*
Supplier differentiation lies in technology and equipment	*Agency differentiation lies in people and processes*

Vendor/Agency differentiation lies in people and processes, not in equipment and technology – A plastic bottle manufacturer distinguishes itself from its competitors by its technology and equipment. Smart buyers sort out the pros and cons of blow molding vs. injection molding, wheel machines vs. shuttle machines, sonic welding vs. spin welding, in-mold labeling vs. post-mold labeling, and so forth. Buyers of manufactured automobile components study continuous casting versus die casting versus evaporative pattern casting. They contrast resin casting with sand casting, each with its own advantages and disadvantages. They look at factory locations, geography, freight and inventory considerations. There is hammer milling and ball milling and dozens of lathing technologies, all of which help differentiate one vendor from the next. In the world of direct materials, suppliers are generally differentiated by technologies and equipment. Buyers can take factory tours and see and touch the differences.

Marketing suppliers differentiate themselves in much more subtle, though equally significant ways. Things like organizational culture, human talent, passion, relatable experiences, and work processes are the great dividers in many marketing sectors. Picking up the differences across agencies takes time and a practiced, discerning eye. One agency may be great at the mass marketing of a single idea, while another one may have a particular sweet spot around communicating health and food related issues to a specific demographic. One agency may be great at targeting their TV advertising to exactly the right audience, while another is outstanding at integrating TV messages with web-based promotions. Yet the newcomer to this space won't discover these critical distinctions by studying agency websites or reviewing responses to standard agency RFIs. And they won't uncover these differences in the first few agency meetings unless they know exactly what to ask the agency and exactly how to ask it.

While direct materials distinctions are fairly static (distinctions are generally derived from capital investments and include high barriers to change), agencies can turn on a dime. An agency can be positioned today as a retail marketing agency, and tomorrow it can reposition itself as a digital agency. Agencies will periodically venture into new areas, and they will quietly and gradually abandon others. Their market is highly fluid. There are low barriers to change. Agency-to-agency differentiation is quite real, but it can be quite hard to detect.

Marketing suppliers are indeed differentiated. But accurately detecting the differences takes specialized skill and experience.

Supplier Qualifications	
Direct Materials Procurement	**Marketing Procurement**
Suppliers are rigorously qualified	*No qualification process*

Direct materials suppliers are rigorously qualified; agencies are, um, well... qualified – If you want to become a qualified supplier of a raw ingredient to a paint company or a pet foods business, you must pass through many rigorous requirements on the way to becoming qualified. You must submit Material Safety Data Sheets and lab samples with standardized chemical analysis data. You must systematically subject your materials to extreme conditions of temperature and humidity and a variety of pressures, and you must provide stability testing data and more analyses. Once you've cleared these steps you submit larger quantities for lab testing. Prospective customers will test your materials for formula compatibility, performance, extended stability, and more. After this, you'll submit even larger batches for production testing and materials handling characteristics, followed by all kinds of long term testing. When you get through all of this, when you finally earn "qualification," you might get the chance to submit a quote and potentially earn business.

Qualifications are a non-existent concept in marketing. That's because there is no "thing" to qualify. The vendor consideration set for the Marketing Procurement person is therefore enormous, sometimes in the hundreds.

Buyers who are new to the marketing space often struggle mightily with this concept. They seem to believe that if they just work hard enough at it, they will be able to create a sort of specification that will ultimately make the agency proposals apples-to-apples. They fail. Worse yet, they miss the point. The real desire is for creative solutions, and that just doesn't lend itself to the concepts of specifications and/or "qualified vendor" lists. We don't want the sourcer that tries heroically to create a specification. We want the sourcer who embraces the fact that specifications don't apply.

Barriers to Entry	
Direct Materials Procurement	**Marketing Procurement**
Suppliers face high barriers to entry/exit	*Suppliers face low barriers to entry/exit*

Because the barriers to entry/exit are so low, supply in marketing services is quite fluid – The world of direct materials is packed with capital-intensive industries. Companies make enormous investments in real estate, facilities, equipment, and technologies. Generally speaking, there are large barriers to entry (and to exit). Paper mills and steel factories don't open and close overnight. Industrial chemical manufacturers and circuit board producers don't jump in and out of markets.

In sharp contrast, agencies become "agencies" when they decide to become an agency. They can become an agency and you can hire them before they have a taxpayer identification number, an office, or a phone. You can walk out to the bus stop and hire a guy sitting on the park bench if he says he's an agency. No governing body will stop you. And just as quickly agencies and marketing suppliers can close their doors and turn off the lights. Though this is a bit of an oversimplification, for the most part, the "business" is just people.

There are some exceptions. Some job-shop type suppliers in direct materials (e.g. manual assembly operations) have low barriers to entry/exit. In marketing there are some examples (e.g. national media agencies, commercial production outfits) that face some serious barriers to entry/exit. But generally speaking, the rule holds.

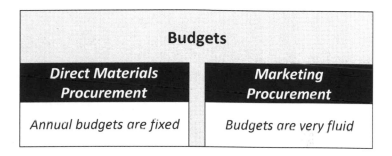

Budgets

Direct Materials Procurement	*Marketing Procurement*
Annual budgets are fixed	*Budgets are very fluid*

Direct materials budgets are fixed; marketing budgets blow with the wind – Most companies fix their production plans at the beginning of each fiscal year, and they lock in their expense budgets accordingly. Buyers (and many others) do forecasts, and budgets are finally built and then cast in cement. They rarely change, and if they do, it is at the end of the fiscal year and the changes are relatively small. Buyers never really have to worry about having enough money to buy what they need to buy.

Because marketing is an elective investment, it is something companies can dial up or down as they see fit. Very often it is the first place to look when times are bad, because it is a discretionary spend. When overall budgets have to be juggled in order to match new business realities, marketing budgets change accordingly. Moreover, the changes can be significant. It is not unusual for television advertisers to unexpectedly and with little warning "go dark" (stop spending altogether) for budgetary reasons. Promotion money can and does get yanked for a variety of reasons. Marketing research gets cut short. Advertising production money gets cut in half with no notice. And just as there can be sudden cuts, there can also be unforeseen windfalls that temporarily flood marketing coffers. All these things happen. All of these things are "normal" in the world of marketing.

Marketing Procurement has to manage agency assignments, contracts, workloads, and relationships in a world where budgets expand and contract.

Marketplace Economics	
Direct Materials Procurement	**Marketing Procurement**
Supply and demand rule marketplace economics	*Marketplace economics are significantly impacted by news, trade press, and media*

The fundamental things that drive marketplace economics are different in the marketing space – A thorough understanding of supply and demand will tell us a lot about marketplace economics in the world of manufactured goods. When capital investment decisions are on the line, suppliers go before their Boards of Directors and review supply and demand data in excruciating detail. Once built, the industry needs to utilize the expensive assets that are in place, and marketplace prices follow. Asset utilization rates and demand patterns can illuminate the future. It may not be an exact science, but in many cases it's close.

The fundamental economics in marketing services is quite different. The basic building blocks of costs are most often people, and facilities come in a distant second. Fixed costs are minimal. And because quality is a variable, one agency's solution isn't necessarily as valuable as that of another agency. Put differently, supply isn't really measureable. Demand is equally un-measureable, and both supply and demand continually surge and decline. The normal laws of supply and demand don't really apply in marketing services.

What does apply in marketing services is something altogether different. It involves much softer considerations, like news, trade publication reports, and the media. One article in a trade journal suggesting that a large advertiser is cutting back its media investment can cause that company's stock to take an instant hit. A media story about how one agency is seemingly on fire, achieving marketing break-throughs at a few of its marquis clients can double demand for that agency's services overnight. A marketer that abuses their agency, that takes advantage of them and treats them unfairly can quickly earn a reputation that drives good agencies away from their doorstep. "We'd love to work with you but we're just too busy right now," the top notch agency will say. The truth will remain unspoken because speaking it could create resentment and the agency could suffer somewhere down the road.

Supply and demand are at play in marketing services, but they move around far more fluidly, and the reasons behind such moves are far more subtle and subjective.

Basic marketplace economics in marketing are far more dynamic, subjective, and difficult to predict than they are in direct materials. What's more, marketing services decisions can have impact that immediately extends to marketplace perceptions about the company, and that can affect things like stock prices in meaningful ways.

Independence vs. Interdependence	
Direct Materials Procurement	*Marketing Procurement*
Each sourcing decision stands alone; decisions are independent	*Each sourcing decision can have big impact on other sourcing decisions; decisions are interdependent*

In marketing, sourcing decisions are interdependent with other marketing sourcing decisions – Let's consider a real-life scenario of a company that makes and sells blank CDs. Somebody buys each of the elements. There is an assembly step. Then somebody sources distribution to the store/retail customer. The finished product finally ends up on the store shelf.

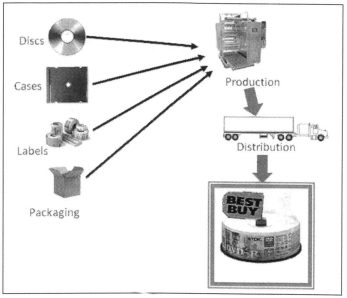

Example of Direct Materials Buying:
Independent sourcing decisions

In this scenario, the buyer of discs can make sourcing decisions based on the disc marketplace. The person buying cases can make sourcing decisions by studying the market for cases. Same for the label buyer, the packaging buyer, the distribution services buyer, and so on. Of course there is some coordination, but their work doesn't really intersect. They really don't need to interact much at all. The label buyer doesn't really have to be concerned with what the disc buyer decides, and the distribution buyer isn't concerned with the sourcing decisions of the case buyer. In some larger companies the individual buyers of various ingredients and materials literally don't know each other, may never have heard of the other buyer, and in the end, don't care. That's not a critique of them or their character. It's a reflection of the reality in direct materials. Direct materials sourcing decisions are independent and they stand alone.

But at the same company, the marketing services buyers operate in a very different environment. Somebody buys ad agency services; somebody buys media; somebody buys digital marketing services; and so forth. Ultimately, the various marketing communications are implemented and they all impact the prospective consumer, who finally arrives at the store shelf and (hopefully) decides to purchase the CDs.

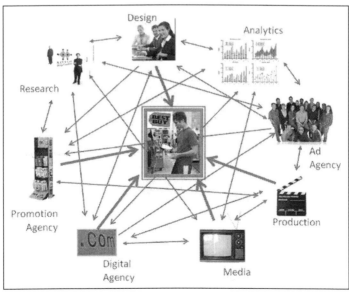

Example of Marketing Buying:
Interdependent sourcing decisions

A decision made by the buyer of design services could impact the Statement of Work (and therefore the sourcing) of a research services supplier. The research services decision could impact how we think about the ad agency services we need, and that in turn can change both the kind of media agency we want and the duration of our contract with the digital agency. Everything has the potential to impact everything else. It's spaghetti. It's all interconnected. Remember, the work does not lend itself to specifications, quality is a variable, and there's nothing that says we have to have a stand-alone promotions agency instead of a one-stop-shop ad agency.

Suppliers in the direct materials world can easily be categorized by commodity. Disc suppliers are disc suppliers. They don't also supply corrugated boxes or shrink-wrap film. They don't dabble in distribution. In marketing, where people (not factories) are the means of production, companies can and do have offerings in multiple areas. An ad agency can indeed offer production services and media services and promotion services and digital services. Or you can buy those pieces separately. But all those sourcing decisions have to be carefully integrated; they have to be managed as a whole.

Sourcing decisions in marketing are highly interdependent.

Ease of Measuring Results	
Direct Materials Procurement	**Marketing Procurement**
It's easy to measure savings	*Measuring results is complicated, imperfect, and subject to skepticism*

Measuring Procurement performance in marketing is imprecise and messy – Because our direct materials expenditures are "costs" and we spend the money grudgingly, savings is the obvious goal and metric. Rightfully so. Measuring savings is pretty straightforward. We usually have a baseline (what we were spending before) and can compare it with what we're spending now, and the resulting difference is clear. In those rare circumstances where we don't have baseline data, for example when we buy something for the first time, there are usually established protocols for assuming or inventing a baseline. Most procurement organizations use the average of the bids or some such standardized methodology. In the world of direct materials the goal is clear, and the numbers are unambiguous and transparent. Metrics and scorecards are straightforward.

Because marketing is an "investment" and not a "cost," and because there are no specifications and therefore no two proposals are the same, savings alone is not a relevant metric. So how should we measure Procurement performance in the context of an investment? Do we estimate future returns and benefits? If so, how much of that should Procurement claim, given all the various groups outside of Procurement that directly contribute to the results? Even if we choose to ignore this question and focus on just measuring savings anyway, we are faced with difficulties. How do we measure something like savings when the various offerings are not apples-to-apples offerings, when each offering is unique? How do we measure savings when the quality being offered is a variable? It's messy at best.

It's important that we don't fall into the obvious trap here, and just default back to good old "savings" as the metric, but many organizations do. It's tempting to think that if the benefits can't be clearly measured, they don't exist. Nothing could be more wrong. That said, measuring Procurement's performance in marketing is "fuzzy."

* * * * *

Net, marketing really IS different. It's different in fundamental and profound ways. It's an investment, not an expense. "Specifications" are nearly impossible to write, and quality is a variable. Buyers can make legitimate sourcing decisions that have impact (good or bad) far beyond the value of the buy. Instead of factories there are people, and that means low barriers to entry/exit and supplier differentiation that is subtle. Budgets bounce around in major ways. Marketplace economics are far more fickle than supply and demand would indicate. Sourcing decisions are interdependent. There is no way to systematically "qualify" suppliers/agencies. Things in general are highly fluid. And measuring Procurement's performance is extremely messy.

From a procurement standpoint, marketing is indeed structurally and inherently different.

So what should we do about that?

5: Okay, Marketing is Different. So What?

To simply say that marketing is different – even to make the case as conclusively and specifically as we just have – is not enough. We need to map out the consequences of those differences and translate those consequences into actionable steps. The fact that marketing is different has big implications for Procurement. The entire playing field is different, and so the approach needs to be different. But before we jump into the specific implications it might be helpful to restate exactly what the marketing space *is*. We've described what it is not. We've detailed how it differs from direct materials. It will be helpful to go one step further, and describe for the Procurement professional exactly what it is.

What the Marketing Environment IS

The marketing environment is people-intensive, creative,

and dynamic. It is a place where relationships are critically important, not because of schmoozing, but because trust is such a bedrock requirement. People aren't creative when they don't feel trusted and valued. Trust is also important because nobody in the mix can rely on systems and processes to keep the ship sailing forward; they instead have to rely on one another. Relational and communications skills are at a premium.

Marketing is highly complex and nuanced, and things are continually evolving. Best practices evolve as new information is learned and new insights are discovered. Because things aren't static, there is no "textbook" that can help the newcomer get fully up to speed. Things have to be learned on the job, and learning never ends. And because there's so much to learn, it takes considerable time. Experience helps.

Marketing is chock full of ambiguity and uncertainty. Because human beings are human beings, and because consumer behaviors depend on a thousand things and are so difficult to predict, the slightest nuances in a marketing plan can make huge differences in the final outcome. The CMO doesn't know if the budgets will change, doesn't know if the agency will deliver breakthrough work, doesn't know if the competitors will reposition their brands, doesn't know if national consumers will follow the behaviors of the test market, doesn't know if the brand will grow or shrink or by how much, doesn't know if the promotion will trigger a consumer call to action or to what degree. These don't represent flaws in the processes of marketing. They reflect the very nature of marketing.

Above all, marketing is something that can have an

enormous impact on the business. Marketing has the potential to launch brands into orbit or to send them the way of the Edsel. That's why companies invest in marketing – because they believe in its power; they believe it grows their business; and they believe it more than pays for itself.

What are the implications for a Procurement organization that wants to succeed in the space we've just described? There are several. Those implications fall into four broad categories: right mindset, right metrics, right skills, and right assignments.

The Right Approach: Four Proven Ways

Right Mindset

In direct materials, Procurement can practice the art of extraction, which is about pulling value from the other guy's pocket and putting it in our pocket. Extract value from them and keep it for us. That takes skill and it's tough to do. It's hardball. It's also the right approach because in direct materials, we are trying to minimize our costs. As long as the items purchased meet our specifications, we should pound on price until the piggy bank breaks. It's a zero-sum game, and we want all we can get.

But that approach is fundamentally different from maximization, which is what is necessary when managing an investment. Maximization is about getting the purchased thing to produce the best results possible in relation to the investment. It's about ROI. Sure, the cost matters. But it matters only in relation to the ultimate yield, the resulting value that is created. In the marketing environment, we need to be thinking about maximization.

If a Marketing Procurement person brings an extraction mindset to this space, he/she will almost always find ways to do it. In contrast to the direct materials world, extraction is actually relatively easy to do in marketing. You just go to the agency and demand they cut their price. They'll whine and complain and agonize. They'll tell others about how awful you are. But then they'll cut their price. The problem is that they can do it a hundred different ways, most of which are hard or impossible to detect, and all of which hurt the end result, the yield, the final return. They can put less hours against the work, or if the hours are monitored, they'll put more junior (less costly) people on various tasks. Instead of doing a customized job on a piece of research, they'll just use syndicated data. Instead of doing a thorough job designing a piece of print creative, they'll pull out an old template and plug in the new words and branding. You'll never know. The procurement person will go claim victory. And the brand and the business will suffer. Don't let the wrong mindset take root in this space; it will cost you.

The right mindset boils down to this: Extraction is out, Maximization is in.

Right Metrics

Rather than addressing deliverables, expectations, or remits, this section focuses on metrics. That's because metrics are more powerful. You can issue the right orders and set the proper expectations, but if you measure the wrong thing, you'll get the wrong thing. Nothing is more certain. This has become a universal truth in management science, and we see examples of it everywhere in Marketing Procurement. CMOs and Procurement leaders say all the right words, but behaviors in the trenches don't change, and that's because the metrics haven't changed.

Marketing isn't an expense line item; it's not a "cost." It's an "investment." It's obvious to everyone that we shouldn't measure an investment by its cost alone. But some will nevertheless say that Procurement should only work on the front end, the cost end; and Marketing is responsible for the outputs, the final sales and equity results to the brands. So keep Procurement focused only on the cost, they argue. Measure them on cost. And measure Marketing on sales and volume. They further rationalize this misguided approach by claiming it will create a healthy tension between Procurement and Marketing. It doesn't. It creates a very unhealthy tension, and it pits one group against the other. It fails. It's a bad idea.

It's as if we choose to invest in a piece of art – let's say a sculpture – by sending Joe off to hire a sculptor and measuring Joe on how low he can get the price; and then measuring Mary by how much the resulting sculpture is worth in the market a year from now. It's an absurd approach, and Joe and Mary will not experience "healthy tension." At best they will resent each other. At worst, they will deliberately work to undermine each other's efforts.

The right metrics for Procurement in this space are the same metrics a CMO might assign to Marketing. We call it *Value Add*. It reflects the idea that we're all working together to improve Marketing ROI. Savings is good. Cost avoidance is good. Incremental profit resulting from incremental sales which result from better marketing is also good. They're all good. Dollars are dollars. All three of these things contribute to improved Marketing ROI. Align Procurement's metrics with Marketing's metrics. Don't settle for making them "complimentary." Don't get talked into making them "simpatico." Make them *identical*.

Be prepared for the immediate, knee-jerk pushback. People don't like measuring what's hard to measure. They will rightly object that measuring the incremental profit from purchased marketing services is very difficult. They will justifiably scream that parsing out a portion of that number – even if you could somehow arrive at it – would be an exercise in arbitrariness. They have a point. But the much bigger point is this: *Don't adopt the wrong metrics because the right ones are messy and hard to do.* Insist on the right metrics; insist on Value-Add. It can be done. I (Gerry) know because I did it. The admitted messiness of the value-add metric has pushed many a Marketing Procurement organization to stick with their old tried-and-true, their good old, comfortable, easy-to-measure, black and white "savings" metric... and their resulting failures are everywhere. The damage they have caused is all over the marketplace.

And then you'll hear this. "Aha!" they will say. "So you mean what we call 'soft savings!' I get it now." No. They don't get it, and we don't mean soft savings. 'Soft savings' is nothing more than the Diet Coke of Savings. In their particular world of Procurement gibberish, Savings is still king. Savings is what's valued. Savings is what matters. Everything else is a lesser-than contribution, a substandard sort of thing, a distant cousin. It will send the message to the

Marketing Procurement people that they are the junior varsity, that this silly "value add thing" isn't as good as the Real Thing: Hard Savings. I know. I lived it. So don't tolerate the term *soft savings*. Insist on the right metric, because metrics will absolutely drive behaviors.

The wrong metric is "savings." Don't let it happen. The right metric is "value-add," and it should drive your Procurement people to want *exactly* the same things as your Marketing people. Measure value-add. Yes, it's tough to do; the right thing often is.

Right Skills

We've already made the case for good strategic sourcing skills, and every CMO should want those skills applied in marketing. Insist on them. If your procurement people don't have these skills, and if you don't hear a clear, coherent reason why the skills they do bring are relevant and valuable to marketing, don't allow them in your area. Marketing is not a good training ground for these skills; it's not a good place for people to learn strategic sourcing on the job. Marketing is too complex; it's too fluid; and the consequences of mistakes are far too painful. When it comes to identifying the right Procurement people for the marketing space, having good, matured, strategic sourcing skills is a given. But that's just the beginning.

The CMO should also insist on people who are comfortable with – and even embrace – uncertainty. The right person doesn't pine for clear boundaries and specifications, doesn't wish for stability and crystal clear deliverables. These things will never, and should never exist in marketing; for if they come in, creativity will go out. The right person doesn't roll her eyes when told to figure out value-add protocols, and she doesn't inch back toward the savings metric because it's straightforward. The right person loves the fluidity of things, the dynamic nature of it, and is energized by the potential she sees in the true nature of this space – in the "messiness" of it. She doesn't try to tame it like a herd of mustangs; she tries to guide it and ride it and, together with her compatriots, tries to make it go where they want it to go.

The right person has great relational and interpersonal skills. The right person doesn't retreat into rules and processes in order to clarify who does what and how things should go. He doesn't set up recurring reports as a way to stay abreast of what's happening in all the various elements of marketing. He doesn't ask the print buyer, the list buyer, the ad agency sourcer, the media buyer, the digital services sourcer, the promotions services sourcer, the design firm buyer, and so on to drive themselves nuts with documentation and structure. Instead he embraces the fluidity and interconnectedness via relationships and collaboration. He's a strategic thinker and a dot connector. What's more, he doesn't force himself to do these things; he does them because they come naturally to him.

The right person is curious and she builds trust with others – with Procurement people, Marketing people, and with agency players. She listens well and by so doing, she communicates respect. As a result, others seek her out and draw her in – they want her involved. She has a low ego. She allows others to claim glory. She adds value and she's a delight to work with.

Sounds a little dreamy, a little over the top, doesn't it? But be careful. Assign a Procurement person who doesn't match these traits into this space, and watch them flounder. They'll struggle because systems and processes don't exist like they do in direct materials. They'll be left out because nobody has to invite them in; there's no way to make their involvement mandatory. They'll miss opportunities because they aren't aware of what's happening in a related area. They'll fail. And the failure won't even be their fault. It will be yours, because you will have put the wrong person in the wrong job. I (Gerry) know. I've done it.

The right person has great strategic sourcing skills, thrives on uncertainty, and has great interpersonal skills. All three aspects are essential. If you don't get all three characteristics, you don't have a good match. If you do find all three, you'll see great things happen.

Right Assignments

After settling on the right metrics and identifying the right candidates for your Marketing Procurement roles, set them up for success by putting them in the right assignment. The right assignment acknowledges the complexity of the space, and it acknowledges the critical importance of the human side of this work.

Learning this space takes time. It takes a lot more time to learn the ropes in marketing than it does in direct materials. That's because of the interconnectedness and the need to understand not just a single spend pool (e.g. commercial production) but also the various related spend pools (e.g. media, general advertising, creative services, research, copy testing, measurement and analytics, direct response, telephone services, etc.). All of these markets are fluid and dynamic. All of these markets are characterized by the elements in the "ten big reasons why marketing is different" section of this book (starts on page 30). It takes a while to learn these markets. Of course you can expect Marketing Procurement people to make contributions very early into their assignment, but mastering the area and finding the biggest opportunities will take them some time.

A second factor here is that relationships take time, too. We're not talking about going to lunch with someone or having them and their spouses over to the house for a New Year's party. We're not talking about getting others to like you. We're talking about trust. In order to be successful, Marketing Procurement people have to be trusted, and that has to be earned. Trust is earned over time by consistently behaving with integrity – that is doing what we say we'll do, by practicing solid interpersonal skills, and by demonstrating courage – and doing it consistently over time. For us to be trusted, people have to believe that we can be counted on to do what we say we'll do, even when it's inconvenient and painful. And that takes time; you don't build real trust overnight. But understand that when a skilled Marketing Procurement person becomes trusted, they become enormously powerful. Their power is not so much a function of rigorous systems and processes and edict (which are less practical in this space); it is the tremendous power of influence, unbounded by systems and processes.

Invest in long term assignments so that people can learn the area and build trust. Your return on this investment will be enormous.

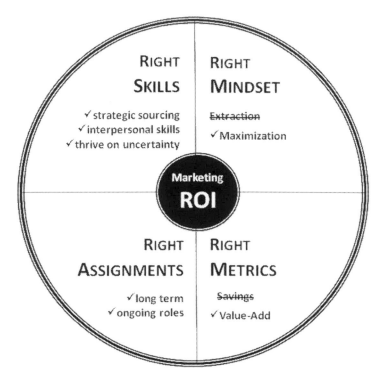

Four Proven Ways for CMOs to Get More for Less

Addressing the Right Audience

Now that we've clarified exactly what's different about the marketing space and clearly defined the implications of those differences, we need to carry this message to the right audience. The right audience is not the Marketing Procurement Foot Soldier, the guy in the trenches who is doing the work. It's not the Marketing Director or the Agency CEO. The right audience is the audience that can bring about the kinds of changes we need. The right audience is the Chief Procurement Officer.

In most organizations, only the CPO can redefine the rules for deciding which person goes into a particular Procurement job, what their mindset needs to be, how they are measured, and the duration of their assignment. We understand that your particular organization might be different. You may have a situation where people other than the CPO can make these things happen. Great. Go work things out with them. The key point here is that the "Marketing Procurement Problem" won't be resolved until and unless we make the foundational changes of right mindset, right metrics, right skills, and right assignments – so we need to be working on those things with whomever can make them happen.

We also realize that in some organizations the CPO will feel like he/she is boxed in. Some CPOs have metrics placed on their shoulders that they are not authorized to change. We know some CPOs are expected to deliver savings, and they feel accountable to the CEO and/or even the Board of Directors. If that becomes an issue, the Chief Financial Officer can often play a very helpful role.

Be Prepared: A Dirty Little Secret

Once we've identified the right player, we need to make the compelling case. We have already laid out the clear and specific reasons as to why the marketing space is different. We've already translated those factors into practical implications that can be acted upon. But there's one other critically important factor in all this. Few people will say it out loud, and it's almost impossible to find someone who will publically admit to this. It's a problem that lurks in the shadows of remote corporate stairwells and little-known, dimly lit tunnels that run under headquarters buildings. It's a cynical notion that's secretly harbored in the hearts of more business leaders than you might ever guess. It's an idea and a belief that gets whispered only in private conversations. And you're the CMO, the last person on earth they'll admit this to. Their dirty little secret is this: *They don't think marketing is a good investment.*

Frustrated by the fact that Marketing is the final holdout in the Land of ROI, skeptical because they have never heard a convincing story about why it's a good idea to invest in marketing, some managers secretly think you should dramatically cut marketing spending back. These aren't a rare few, low-level oddballs. We have had such conversations with CFOs, CPOs, and VPs. They don't see the evidence and they simply don't think it pays out. Although marketing doesn't lend itself to the kind of rigorous ROI analyses that can be done on capital investments or things like R&D, these skeptics interpret not having ROI data as an indicator of guilt. The reason all this is important is because these people don't even accept our basic premise. They resist the idea that marketing is an investment and not a cost. They resist the idea that we should try to maximize the investment because they secretly see the "investment" as actually being a "cost." Once they adopt this cynical view, they see "savings" as the only way to go.

CMOs must be prepared to address this phenomenon directly, and they have to detect the subtleties that mark its presence. The best way we've found to make the case for marketing as an investment is in research done by Professor

John Philip Jones, who is recognized as a leading expert on the economics of advertising. In one of his early works, he studied the impact of advertising on long term share growth, among other things. He found that advertised brands (includes the full bell curve of everything from great ads to terrible ads) outperform unadvertised brands by 6%. And brands with great advertising (top quintile of ad quality) outperform unadvertised brands by 32%. Further, he finds that good ads, when combined with media continuity and above average promotional expenditure outperform unadvertised brands in long term share growth by 50%.[7]

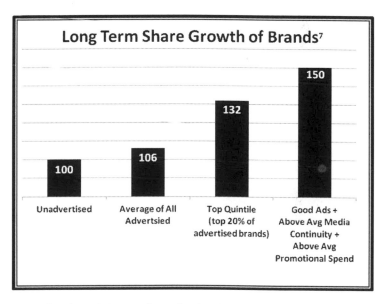

Proof: Advertising and marketing investments grow brands

---

[7] See *When Ads Work: New Proof That Advertising Triggers Sales*, by John Philip Jones, 1995. Published by Lexington Books, an imprint of The Free Press, Simon & Schuster, Inc. Cited data is derived from pages 23 and 210 in this first edition work.

Some in the marketing world prefer other ways of making the case that marketing works, that it's a good investment. Use whatever way works for you. But be aware, what you take for granted – that marketing is a worthy investment – is not something everyone takes for granted. And we have to tackle this misconception before we can make the rest of our case.

Going Forward

We give the following direction with a sense of something akin to embarrassment and humility. It is so simple, so obvious, so unsophisticated. And yet we can count on one hand the number of cases in which this has actually been done. Evidence piles up every day in the marketplace, and that evidence begs for a thousand more of these conversations. Making the right case to the right audience means sitting down with the CPO and delivering a convincing message:

1. Confirm a foundational understanding that marketing is a good investment
2. Explain in detail why marketing is a unique space (the ten reasons from Chapter 4)
3. Describe the implications (right mindset, metrics, skills, assignments)
4. Get agreement and get going.

Of course there are additional good practices and techniques in this area, and we'd be happy to discuss them with you at length. But if you just stay focused on the above basics, you'll see breakthroughs that will put a smile on your face. We promise.

When engaged in the proper way, Procurement players with good strategic sourcing skills can help you grow Marketing ROI. You really get more for less, and they can help.

Appendix: The Case for Consultants

Throughout this book, we have emphasized that the goal is improving ROI and that engaging strategic sourcing skills in the right ways can help CMOs succeed. We've made the point that it's not about engaging Procurement; it's about engaging the skills. Some procurement organizations have these skills and they are great at practicing them. Some procurement organizations are still developing the skills, and there are ways for them to get better. Another alternative for the CMO is to engage these skills via outside consultants, such as through so-called search firms, like External View Consulting Group. Self serving? Sure, but that's not why we're presenting this option. We are presenting the option because it can sometimes be a very good one for CMOs whose internal Procurement groups don't have the requisite capabilities. But we're also going to go a step further. We're going to describe why search consultants can sometimes be even better than a good internal Marketing Procurement Team.

But first, the negatives. Consultants are not a good long term option because they tend to be "in-and-out" players. It is preferable to have skilled people in place for an extended assignment, as discussed earlier. They also have to learn a company's internal systems and culture before they can be fully effective. By contrast, internal players will already have a handle on those things, and they will have an ongoing inherent advantage over an outsider.

Now the positives. There are six good reasons why search consultants deserve to be in a CMOs consideration set. Search Consultants have big, inherent, structural advantages over internal Procurement organizations. To illustrate the points, I (Gerry) will compare my experience at the world's largest marketer with my experiences on the consultant side.

Good search consultants consistently apply good strategic sourcing skills – This was a pleasant surprise for me when I left the corporate nest and immersed myself into the world of consultants. A few years ago P&G was named the Procurement Organization of the Year, and I was personally part of P&G's response to an investigative effort by *Purchasing* magazine to assess our methods and practices. I'm proud of that heritage and of P&G's procurement excellence in general. That's why I was so surprised when I later discovered how good some consultancies were at strategic sourcing. Consultants sometimes use different terminology, but good ones indeed apply solid, fundamental sourcing processes and techniques. Their approach is thoughtful, penetrating, strategic, and built on a foundation of profound market knowledge. Their processes and methods are excellent and their applications strike the right balance between process rigor and appropriate flexibility. Good search consultants have good strategic sourcing skills.

Search consultants do more and go deeper because they have more time to do strategic sourcing and search - While inside the P&G system, I had to deal with many organizational and internal issues that distracted me from the work of sourcing. Not by a little bit; by a lot. This is a problem for every Procurement group, whether it be at GlaxoSmithKline or Visa or Aflac or GM. By contrast, search consultants wake up in the morning, and do sourcing work all day long, every day. No personnel issues. No quarterly reviews. No two-day, offsite, leadership team meetings. No office relocations or personnel ratings meetings or sponsorship sessions or budget debates or meetings where you just don't need to be. Just sourcing.

These things aren't failures on the part of marketers or clients. They are organizational necessities, part of what it takes to run large companies. These things are appropriate. But they are *structural* and seriously hamper the time an internal player can spend on the real work of Marketing Procurement. When I was on the "inside," I met with dozens of agencies every year. By contrast, a good search consultant (Russel) proved to me that he met with over two hundred agencies in the last twelve months. There's just no comparison.

Search Firms do the work with more experienced, senior people - While at P&G I oversaw the sourcing, the search, the procurement work for many areas of marketing, including media, interactive, promotion, PR, design, and more. The simple truth is that it was very hard for me to be directly involved; much just had to be delegated. Too often, the people doing the front-line work were light on experience. Great people, very bright, and I love and respect them to this day. But it's not the same as having a twenty-year veteran doing the work, meeting agency executives and penetrating thorny issues. Good search consultants are doing the work with real veterans. Most principles at these consulting firms have been doing agency search work for roughly twenty years. Good search consultants know more agency and client people – really know them – than I ever could have from the inside.

Search consultants have a broader perspective, seeing across a wider range of clients and client industries - While at P&G, I reached out to McDonald's, Coca-Cola, Eli Lilly, Seagram's, M&M Mars, Anheuser-Busch, plus a few more. These forays into their worlds ranged from a single phone conversation to a few face-to-face meetings. These sessions were helpful and they felt good. They gave me a broader perspective on the agency marketplace. What about search consultants?

Each year External View alone sees *in depth* across at least ten industries and across dozens of clients. Consultants see clearly the things that industries and clients have in common, and the things that make them unique. Ironically, they even saw P&G more clearly than I did, because I simply didn't have the broader context. I couldn't truly see P&G's distinctiveness vs. auto companies, QSR's, retailers, etc. the way they did. The fact that P&G is a promote-from-within place made this even tougher for me. Again, P&G

wasn't/isn't wrong. But there are structural differences that give search consultants an advantage, and their rich exposure to many advertisers and client industries is a big one.

Search consultants see many more agencies, and especially when they pitch and when they service clients - I got to see many agencies pitch P&G and then saw how they did against delivering on their promises. But my exposure was very narrow in comparison to what the search consultant sees. Week after week, month in and month out, consultants see agencies make promises and then deliver – or fail. They see it over and over, across different clients and different business situations. They simply have a richer perspective on who agencies are, on how they pitch, on how they perform, and how they handle gaining or losing business. Search consultants don't know agencies just by reading their promotional packet. They visit them and see them present their capabilities, see them win or lose, and see them perform on the assignments they win. Structurally, I just couldn't do that to any comparable extent from inside a marketing company.

Search consultants have more clout - P&G was and is the biggest advertiser in the U.S. (and in the top five globally) and that meant a lot when I went to meet with agencies and marketing vendors. I used to look at the Ad Age roster of advertisers and assess my clout accordingly. But now I better understand how search consultants accumulate major clout from their many clients. Of course they don't leverage dollars directly (i.e. don't combine volumes to behave as a consortium buyer). But the annual spend that they represent is still nevertheless very large, and the strategic importance of the businesses they represent is a very big deal to agencies and marketing vendors. Clout at P&G was all about size and dollars and scale, about going out there with one huge demand – and P&G has been great at it. In terms of annual business volumes, search consultant clout comes close to that of the largest marketers in terms of size and scale. But the real leverage is in knowledge, familiarity, repetition and strategic significance. The foundation of this clout is personal integrity and credibility, which can only be built over years and across a multitude of interactions.

* * * * *

Net, because search consultants are out there in the market all the time, because they represent many attractive clients and large spends, and because they have a deep base of knowledge, they can do everything I could do as an insider, plus more. They have structural advantages that give them valuable perspective, and they can be an excellent choice for a CMO who wants to leverage good strategic sourcing skills.

Additional Resources

External View Consulting Group advises marketers on all aspects of agency management, and is available to discuss your specific situation. We offer consultative services in a number of areas, including agency search, ongoing agency management and relationship optimization, and development of effective Marketing Procurement organizations.

www.Ext-ViewGroup.com
9925 Jefferson Blvd.
Culver City, CA 90232

Gerry Preece
GerryP@Ext-ViewGroup.com
513-225-0242

Russel Wohlwerth
RusselW@Ext-ViewGroup.com
310-841-4502

38923330R00049

Made in the USA
Middletown, DE
30 December 2016